Epicanthus

poems by

Hiromi Yoshida

Finishing Line Press
Georgetown, Kentucky

Epicanthus

*For my mother, Dr. Toyoko Yoshida,
and my sister, Tama Lang,
who stood with me on every wavering
epicanthic threshold.*

Copyright © 2021 by Hiromi Yoshida
ISBN 978-1-64662-660-1 First Edition
All rights reserved under International and Pan-American Copyright Conventions. No part of this book may be reproduced in any manner whatsoever without written permission from the publisher, except in the case of brief quotations embodied in critical articles and reviews.

ACKNOWLEDGMENTS

Grateful acknowledgment is made to the editors of these publications in which these poems first appeared, sometimes in different versions.

The Asian American Literary Review, "NYC Chinatown"
Discover Nikkei, "She Remains," "Godwind," "Umami," "Googling Monika"
Evening Street Review, "TV Dinner"
Fine Wine Mortar: A Matrix Anthology of Literary and Visual Arts, "Chinese Lantern"
Flying Island, "Shikata ga Nai (Let It Be)," "Hiroshima & Nagasaki"
Gidra, "COVID America," "The Lunchbox," "Grandmother's Kitchen"
Spirit Fire Review, "Mother's Garden"

Publisher: Leah Huete de Maines
Editor: Christen Kincaid
Cover Art: Detail from untitled photograph, Tokyo Noir Series,
           Hiromi Yoshida, photographer (different from author),
           www.hiromiphotography.com
Author Photo: Toyoko Yoshida
Cover Design: Elizabeth Maines McCleavy

Order online: www.finishinglinepress.com
           also available on amazon.com

Author inquiries and mail orders:
Finishing Line Press
PO Box 1626
Georgetown, Kentucky 40324
USA

Contents

Epicanthus 1
NYC Chinatown 2
Moon Palace King 4
Shikata ga Nai (Let It Be) 6
Hiroshima & Nagasaki 7
Japanese War Brides 8
Godwind 14
Gas Panic 15
Collateral Damage 16
COVID America 17
Chinese Lantern 20
Fortune Cookie 21
The Lunchbox 22
The F-Word 23
Empire State Building Soup 24
Hot Lunch 25
TV Dinner 26
Bologna 27
The Mouse 28
Grandmother's Kitchen 29
Channel Surfers 30
She Remains 31
Mother's Garden 32
Umami 33
Wei-Wei's Gift 34
Googling Monika 35
Additional Acknowledgments 36

Epicanthus

curvilinear fold
enveloping the Asiatic
eye, liminal

barrier [Caucasoid |
Mongoloid]

the sly difference
winks; the epithelial rim
of the *petit objét* a
seduces the Lacanian

voyeur into complicity with the obese

        camel lumbering through the glinting eye
                of the epicanthic needle.

NYC Chinatown

Mei-Mei and I dragged heavy, weary feet down Chinatown sidewalks—
boredom skewing our colorful Macy's dresses, summer smearing
empty hands. Our busy mouths melted rice paper chewing

Botan candy pulp, sticky be-
tween
tiny
teeth. We dawdled and waited—
waited and dawdled,
for Mama to determine weight of lichees,
price of ginger roots (when we loved

Libbyland TV dinners,
especially the frozen
peas
you stick
on every
fork
prong).

We wanted Papa to end his endless talk with the grocery store owner
in some language we didn't know behind stacks of Chinese newspapers
and cigarette cartons and dried ginseng and Tiger Balm jars.

It looked like our whiny wish would come true, and we'd be entertained
when the stranger
outside the store said, "Hello," with a stringy smile. (Wow! He

sounds like Mr. Sulu!) "Hey,
I want to show
you something. It's over
there, come on."

(Well… He doesn't look like the
Bogeyman and he didn't offer us candy). So, Mei-Mei and I trailed after
Mr. Stringbean
with the long hair falling into chinky eyes and the friendly American
voice striding block
after block to ghastly

green-painted tenement
doorway.
"It's behind this door."

I poked cautious
head around

curious corner; eyes spied
pint-sized Tropicana
orange juice carton
smashed onto dirty
tiled floor.

Spread-eagle upsweep—
jack-be-nimble fingers smeared
shame between dangling legs.

"Where's your sister?
Stay right here." I

dared not budge from that
dirty green place. Thick

moths dropped
in the doorway.

Debris of dusk gathered
beneath hairy doormats.

Buzzards ate dogs.

My caged heart
beat flyaway
chickencoop feathers; Runaway

little sister, runaway from
scary yucky chinky guy—run back to Mama and Papa at the grocery store;

fold all thoughts away
(carefully, very carefully)

like today's crumpled
yellow dress—slip through Chinese
laundry steam—it's suddenly
such an easy feat to

stick
frozen
peas
on
every
fork
prong.

Moon Palace King

He shrivels into mummy-
sized coffin dimensions, like a
secretly decaying tooth
in the mouth of Time—festering into
the moon's halitosis, porous and
respectable, sporting Prufrock's
askew neckties—unraveling in
the heavy direction that gravity loves. We

never had a strong common language,
despite the black hair and high cheekbones
we shared genetically—just the child's
Japanese tripping off my stuttering

tongue. I'd never understood
his need for three consecutive wives
(anachronistic exorbitance)—Mother being
sloppy seconds to the unknown
first, angelically dead. Third wife's
deal was the worst of all—she'd felt
coerced to kiss the behind of some leering devil
that winked at her in a moth-eaten universe. Today,

Father is the gold-toothed mummy—
Don Giovanni of amorphous days
in New York City, king of Moon Palace restaurant
on Broadway & West 112th Street near
Columbia University, where all the Beat Generation
guys did their beatific thing equally sloppily;
and the pink crocuses bloomed each spring
on sidewalk islands; and the grey-
haired shopping bag lady howled beneath
the painted building façade reading:

"The wages of sin is death
But the gift of God
Is eternal life
In Jesus Christ, Our Lord."

Father was also the Taiwanese Malcolm X
whose family name was an overused signifier
in the buzzing silence wake of slammed-
down phone receivers on crackling,
cacophonous death threats for supporting Taiwan
during the Nixon years. He was

the lean, sinewy man in the white
wife beater shirt,
who flung open
the window sash to yell,
"*Bakayarō!*"
at upstairs neighbors pounding piano
keys in the humid New York City night;

who playfully struck the back of
my head when I'd switched on the fixtured ceiling lights in
my Burgess Hall bedroom
in glaring daylight hours;

who yelled at me, Mother, and Mei-Mei
for Charmin toilet paper overuse (when a taut, blackened
public rope had served that function for him
in rural Tainan);

who instructed me and Mei-Mei to repeat
after him, "*Zhōnghuá mínguó wànsuì!*"
and wave our little ROC flags;

who embarrassed me by speaking broken
English to my American playmates;

whose long lean hand spooned syrupy apricot mush into the
open giggling mouth of my baby sister;

NYC childhood memories of undivorced Father remain—
vaguely colored streamers from the heart's broken
piñata—bandages unraveling from the mummified feet of Time.

Shikata ga Nai (Let It Be)

Stoic acceptance

      - not passive acquiescence
      - not dumb cattle herded into packed boxcars
      - not subservient Japs (as

          though truncation diminishes self-esteem)—

swallowing the bitter spittle
of outrage re. E.O. 9066
like green tea without the usual
ceremony.   Heavy steps   overstuffed duffel bags—

all that two arms can carry
(all that the heart can carry)

Shikata ga nai.   Swallow, lunge   forward

gravel   crunch [toxic *gaman*]

overblown chrysanthemum heads drop
      with the weight of
      apology ["*mōshi wake nai*"] for being

Japanese Americans at the wrong time (as
  though there were a right time for these   porous   hybrid
          many-petaled things)—
The skies above Manzanar were sheets of moth-eaten kimono silk—
    taut with anxiety, mottled with unanswered questions, pinpricked with
cruel stars;

The lacquered *bento* boxes
The *sake* cups
The porcelain rice bowls
The spoons, the chopsticks,
     the *obi* sashes matchless with lost kimono   pieces   and the children
        without their *Hinamatsuri* dolls (where are they now?)

Cucumbers and   plums pickle in formaldehyde   jars

Shikata ga nai.

Hiroshima & Nagasaki

The flash

The crash

The ash.

Decimation was instantaneous—skeletons etched upon asphalt,

                shadows sick with radiation

                            vomited skyward curses—

The True Man hanging from the over-blossoming

tree of public panic   unlynched.

Japanese War Brides

"They're Bringing Home Japanese Wives,"
Smith & Worden warned the nation
in the January 19, 1952 issue of *The Saturday Evening Post*.

This postwar shift in American demographics
Was really the result of pornographics:
Butterfly mamas with dumpling tits
Bodacious geishas with pidgin toes
Godzilla girls with bazooka eyes
Kimono dolls with slanty panties
Pan-Pan gals with red-lacquered lipstick
Origami schoolgirls with pleated skirts
Hello Kitty virgins with cherry blossom nipples;
America's orientalist dream factories
Operated overtime beyond the vested reaches—
Of national interest.

So, let's dream of long and happy days—
Of happy housewives smiling in gingham dresses, and white pinafore aprons
And Norman Rockwell girls with Raggedy Anns and Mary Janes
And Wonder Bread boys with chocolate chip freckles peering over—
   whitewashed fences:
At the milkman and the Tin Man
The Candy Man and the bandy man
The Pillsbury Doughboy and the dingleberry snowboy
And Chef Boyardee with the big fat spaghetti-O's
And Mister Clean with the hoop earring
And Mrs. Jones with the curling pin
And Sally with the tinseled tutu
And the Green Giant with the beanstalk sprouting—
   from Jack's cracked flowering beanpot head.

After all, these Japanese women
Threaten to contaminate the gene pools
Of American wonderland.
Our big beneficent boisterous land
Of big beefy cattle and big steel mills
And speckled eggs and golden apples
And endless milkyways
And running creeks and dappled trout
And waves of corn and wheat and barley

And the Rocky Mountain range of sky and stars and multi-tiered shelves of rock
 formation and eagles
  swooping—
   down giddy heights
    into purple canyons of   endless haze

This great land of Sunkist earth and star-spangled sky
Will shrink and wilt and breed

A specious species
Of diminutive yellow bonsai dwarfs
Sprout black pubic hair
And pigeon toes
And mottled skin
(Buck teeth
Knock knees
Cross eyes
Small cock)

Not to mention—
American squish cheese
And cooties from
 the Bogie Man lurking around
 Johnny-come-lately's house.

These Japanese women can't make coffee
Cook Spam or mold Jell-O
Bake loaves or roll meatballs
Count teaspoons or measure ounces
(Thanksgiving will be a Turkish disaster!)
They'll burn your toast
They'll scorch your eggs
They'll crack your plates
Bust your balls
Break your heart
And bleed you dry
(Rice paddy leeches).

What's more, these foreign wives will
Pickle your plums and cabbage leaves
Pour soy sauce into your coffee maker

Add Drano to your washing machine
Squirt Fantastik on your clothes
Drop mothballs into your chicken soup
Stitch eyes on the heads of Raggedy Anns
And giggle at the spastic antics
Of your arthritic mother.

For God's sake marry
A reg'lar American gal
With big white boobs and endless legs
And Hollywood dimples
And starry eyes
(And consummate turkey, amen!)
She'll give you the sparkle of big blue Lakes
And flowers of the Rocky Mountain range
Between spread-eagle thighs
A Miracle Whip
Of Six Flag adventure
And Ferris wheel rides
And Candyland canes

And Ivory Snow babes with golden curls
And gingerbread boys with cinnamon eyes
And candy-striped girls with popcorn balls
   dipping Girl Scout cookies into cherry vanillas.
Wish upon a twinkling star
And catch the moon in your baseball glove.

But what about the dream of a thousand nights
In secret bamboo groves
And flowering drumsongs
And almond eyes
And silky sayonaras
Ending happily-ever-after
And paper moons and burning lanterns
And incense coiling will-o'-the-wisps—
Slipping through tents of mosquito net
And fireflies weaving a drunken dance
Gentle tattoo of rain
And mist
  hanging

From temple eaves.

Japan, this quilted land of Zen epiphanies
And vermillion carp and gingko trees
And persimmon shimmering
In kimono sleeves—
Sprawled a devastation
And a winding trail
Of Hiroshima ash
And broken ancestral bone
Buried with stone tablets
And gold calligraphies
And a million sutras
Of suns and moons and Lotus lands of light
And the wailing weeping mothers
Cradled their loss in stunted arms

While GI Joes gave out chocolate bars
And baseball bats
And Band-Aid strips
And vaguely wonderous American dreams
To Keiko and Hanako and Teruko:
Gold mines and diamond rings
Color TVs and silver screens
White bathroom tiles and kitchen appliances
Betty Crockery and singing sewing machines
And fields of flowers
And seas of stars
And a soft tumble—
   Into the fragrant hay.

They fed her white lies (she says)
Gave blue-eyed injections
With overloaded stun guns—
And sour milk and rotten apples
Thistledown and nettle sting
Cactus flower and piney prickle
Broken trinkets and tarnished rhinestone
And a racist mother-in-law.
For the sloppy Joes who bring home their Japanese brides,
Grueling rice and sticky pudding

Incompatible condiments cause indigestion
A diarrhea for the nation
And a pancreas pancake
Of ulcerous gallstone
And a jumping bean dance
Of squinty tapeworm.

So what?
If they're bringing home Japanese wives
Happy housewivery is knavery
Tomfoolery and slavery,

An importation of labor
(Disguised as marriage)
For suburban consumption
And small-town talk.
If Smith & Worden had informed the nation
"They're Bringing Home European Wives,"
Readers would've demanded
Tabloid news—
Something weird and downright outrageous.
European imports
(brides included) are
Part and parcel—no strings attached—
Of laissez-faire
And national trust
And rising stocks
And corporate estimates
Of USCIS statistics
And population growth
To "Make America Great Again."

In other words,
The normal course
Of labor migration
In the Department of Reproduction
(also known as Immigration)
Is a Mayflower route
Across stormy seas—
A maiden voyage
Into the unknown—

Howling Injun desertscapes
Of our brave New World
Of black-eyed-susans
And pilloried dreams
Rather than
A Silk Road trail
Stealing across Pacific seas

With suspect cargo
And cryptic bills of lading:
Bales of rice
And chicken cages
And berry-berry and weevils
And chinamen
With lopsided pigtails,
All replete with eunuch smiles.

Despite these histories
Of transatlantic victory
And transpacific duplicity
What is the big deal
About Japanese women
And their eternal mystique—
An orientalist construct,
A pulpy fantasy narrative?

Japanese war brides
Remain with us
A legacy of immaculate survival
Beneath the skies of suture
And nirvana light—
Bleaching a cremation
Of fire and marrow—
The phoenix forever rising
From Hiroshima ash.

Godwind

The planes deliberately collided into the World
Trade Center, North and South Towers,
like steel-winged Icarus, twinned, burning—

kamikaze crash and decimation—the shredded paper gods shedding green
    pennies and white hair—the Manhattan skyline was a smoggy plexiglass
altar
where dreams were
        sacrificed to the rising sun (that smirking bastard). Pedestrians
coughed, gagged on

the foretaste of phoenix ash; black stench
of needless apocalypse clogged
    nostrils—resurrection an unwritten blueprint drifting on wayward
godwind—

Gas Panic

Inhaling the same toxic air—
            ominous shift of carbon molecules
in Hibiya line subway cars—morning
commuters held in
       the nausea (gag reflex)

ignoring beckoning silk Hanae Mori
handkerchiefs; contact lenses shriveling
    like oversized fish scales in reddening eyes;
manicured fingertips fluttering toward disheveling
        hair—cell phones sinking in deep pockets—

briefcases dropping—soft sleepy slump of
bodies ["*Tasukete kudasai!*" unstated,
"*Iie, daijōbu desu,*" contending]—nylon ladders stretching down
           panty-hosed legs—high heels breaking
into staccato runs—toward diminuendo of public trust—

allegedly, first responders are never
bystanders in Tokyo, and Japanese commuters are
perfect bioterrorism victims; both apathy and courtesy are
paralyzing: How can tacitly implicit privacy barriers be
penetrated without shattering plexiglass selves into a million
carbon molecules? After all, self-

truncation in Japan is like an amputated
yakuza pinky, literal *yubi-kiri*,
kamikaze self-sacrifice to Shinto gods—blood pact,
and childhood promise of a thousand needles swallowed—
            a crinkling shrinkage of cringing selves,
giftwrapped in polyester *furoshiki*. The corporate gift

of permanent service to the *kaisha* had unraveled that volatile morning of
umbrella-point-punctured liquid sarin sacks—devotion to Aum Shinrikyo
being a toxic alternative—

and after Shoko Asahara's execution, he bloated into the *yubi-kiri* pinky,
amputated public promise.

Collateral Damage

That bleeding child—
cradled in the smiling firefighter's arms;
preciously preserved for burial; salvaged
from the Alfred P. Murrah Building's debris mountain—
"collateral damage," she was called (slaughter
of the innocents). In her little green
grave she has slept since 1995,
undamaged spirit,
Pulitzer Prize glory for that accidental
photograph; glow-worms gleam
in the black-and-white ash
heap of photogenic smiles each April
of cruel glory, and we remember
the Oklahoma City National Memorial site,
now "temporarily closed" by COVID-19.

COVID America

It began with the "Chinese virus"—injected invective into mainstream
    media flows—no filters—till the United States of America became

a filthy petri dish—breeding, incubating resurrected #hashtags and multiple trun-
cations, shutdowns, lockdowns, one-

handed masturbation sessions—Walmart shopping sprees for toilet paper
and hand sanitizer—6' apart isn't long enough distance between Democrats
and Republicans—
the length of an average-sized coffin in America. And now,

masked faces are politically correct emojis, and schoolchildren and teachers
are collateral damage, waiting to be counted and collected—slipping through
the cracks of the
2020 census,

while Karen became the princess ensconced in ice at the glassy apex of
Capitol Hill, and George Floyd became the summer #hashtag erupting from
claustrophobic suburban closets. If the coronavirus is a

left-wing government hoax, then, the KKK is a masquerade of sadomasochistic
Blacks, smirking in white hoods.

Halt TikTok negotiations because no American's got a "chinaman's chance."
Swallow bleach to sanitize mansions of the mind inundated with misinformation—
Pimp Polaroids for Facebook Likes and Twitter followers—
Keep digging in the gold mines of overflowing
    dumpsters with rubber gloves—pick out soggy Cheerios with OCD
childhood spoons (because all lives matter in Heaven & Hell).

A COVID test is like a Shirley Jackson lottery, but the black dot is the cue ball
shot across vast green fields where stripes and solids, and life and death, are
equal opportunities [for all].

America, the big-boobed nation, is not particularly interested in flattening
out curves—because bigger is better, and Biggest is Best. So, let's go ahead,
and say that COVID-19 is symptomatic of the American diseases of:

- racism (and all other 'isms and orgasmic schisms)
- corporate greed
- homelessness
- obesity

sugar, salt, butter, cheese, red meat, fast food, barbecue sauce overkill—
Mrs. Butterworth, Uncle Ben & Aunt Jemima, the ménage-à-trois falling off their respective supermarket shelves like shot-down Confederate statues. And BLM is

the graffiti scrawl
of underground discourses like the N-word, the F-word, the word branded upon the obscene, obese flesh of the (denying, white) American brain; the Word with which the world began (and could end). So,

cover up the Big American Motor Mouth (speak no evil)—
spitting out epithelial epithets—using leftover duct tape from 9-11 terror alert days;

Fauci & Kevorkian morph into siamese twins in paranoid collective consciousness—
in a nation ruled by old white men.

When will Uncle Sam wear a dress? (when he/she/they are dressed to kill?)
When will we cry uncle?
When will Mother know best?
When will entropic atoms coalesce into utopia?

Nobody in America wants to wear a mask
that covers up full, luscious, smiling lips (Cover Girl disenfranchised).

Nobody wants to comply
with government mandates in a democratic America—a gag bag of party tricks; a piñata exploding plastic Cracker Jack prizes in your face.

America is an immigrant's wet dream—
the green residue of pinched pennies.

America is a melting pot of
incompatible condiments—a conundrum of pundits;
lamb stew of Crab Rangoons and national lampoons; Willy Wonka's

chocolatier wok,
and Charlie Chan's ChapStick factory—

enigmatic reduction of USPS operations—
generates nostalgia for the taste of glue on the sticky backsides of US postage stamps.

America is a silly thing,
America is a bleached-blonde virago.
"America" is a floating signifier—
Hollywood's mega-mouth "sound & fury."

America is a masquerade of giggling, scrawny, pimpled, dimpled teenagers.
America is a narcissist, reflected in gilt-edged, gargantuan, baroque mirrors—
guilt-tripping down strip malls—stripped of all shame, like the naked Emperor.

American dads curse at barbecue grills that won't start up;
American moms upbraid their pigtailed daughters for smashing their overstuffed piggy banks prematurely—
American kids vie for the biggest unbroken cookie;
American dogs sniff the biggest crotches.

And it all ends with the "Chinese virus"—eating its own grey spermatozoic rat-tail uroborically—gagging on the dust of desecrated Edens—shriveled mummy Chinatowns scattered across the pock-marked moon face of America; the Polaroid cheese that stands
alone on one shriveled Zen leg.

Chinese Lantern

dragon trapped in cylindri-
cal sea devours red tail
coiling round prismatic gilt-
edged dream chambers
mist clambering steep
banks drift sleep endless
cloud cataract break

flower formation undulate
celestial turquoise smoky
jade bead heavy amber hours
psychedelic hemorrhage

behind papered eyes

Fortune Cookie

Tease out the papered secret from the
vulval crevice—cryptic stream like
Lotto numbers, but Joy-Luck instead.

The Lunchbox

Second-grade lunchtime,
my metallic
lunchbox latch
snaps open—
jack-in-
the-box quease—
peek-a-boo, I
see the glinting
hint of some-
thing brown, viscous,
cold, pungent,
speckled red.
Only the rice was
recognizable. Chop
suey goo oozing secret
anticipation—sweating noonday
hunger, until the buzzards
of doubt began their awk-
ward squawk. "Ugh…
What is that?" My
classmates poked
freckled pug
noses around the
corner of my lunchbox
to glimpse a
glint of the
dubious goo I'd
wanted to hide.
"Nothing," I
closed the lunchbox lid,
and indeed my
Chinese lunch was a
viscous void,
unnamable,
unlike peanut butter
and jelly oozing delight
from porous Wonder
Bread slabs.

The F-Word

Brett sat sullen across from me
        in second-grade social studies class,
                like an empty Humpty Dumpty. He

squished a
tiny paper
bit into a
grey snot-
sized ball—rolled it across desk surface in my direction.

Unfolded,
I saw
an unknown
word. I
balled that
dirty paper
bit, and

gingerly placed it
        on Allison's clean desk surface.

Again unfolded,
Allison's green eyes
dilated, glinted—her arm flailing upward:

"Mrs. Santa Barbara,
Hiromi gave me
this!" That yucky thing
        in the homeroom teacher's graceful, quizzical hands—
                opened like a dirty, enigmatic origami piece. Mrs. Santa Barbara, who had
                      praised my prose description of pure white snow falling on rooftops,

asked me in a syrupy sweet voice: "Do you know what this word means?"

"No, Ma'am. Brett gave it to me."

Seeds of
knowledge were
hard, unsprouted

kernels in my puzzled
head; the second-grade classroom a
                public urinal tribunal that dirty afternoon.

The Empire State Building Soup

Hot water spurt—
scalding cataract, hiss
of disappointment—
into the void of
that metallic place
where the paper
cup should have
dropped. I

gaped at the steam,
the yellowish
inane water for
chicken soup gurgling
down the pipeline
of a malfunctioning
vending machine
on the observation
deck of the Empire State
Building, over-
looking the silvery
panorama of yellow
taxicabs crawling

along W. 34th
St., diligent ants I
wanted to smash
like the undropped
soup cup.

Hot Lunch

Pale yellow plastic
St. Hilda's cafeteria hot lunch trays
mocked steaming aluminum foil TV dinners:
dubious dank green mess of over-
boiled spinach; cold mound of unseasoned
mashed potatoes; smear of butter on half-
slices of white bread; jiggling dark brown glop of
chocolate pudding [where's the beef?]—memories

evaporate, coalesce, like steam with no power
to scald.   Grab the half-pint carton of
chocolate milk before all other

greedy child hands; get tangled in the scraggly
hag hair of time.

TV Dinner

Snowbound nights my PhD-seeking mom
decided to give herself a break; and me,
and Mei-Mei a treat, I relished
each steaming Swanson TV dinner item, nestled
in crinkled aluminum foil, an American *obento* box:

Veal parmigiana meatloaf
    smothered in tomato sauce and mozzarella cheese;
Mashed potatoes,
    fluffy white and buttery yellow;
Green peas,
    ultimate food for kids
to play with;

        Apple strudel,
      central dessert delight,
       ensconced in tiniest
aluminum square,
beckoning
    baked jewel, apple of
      my hungry eye.

Nothing compared to Mom's
oven-baked Scotch eggs, of
course, but those TV

dinners enabled me and my baby
sister to see
who could stick

a
pea
on
every
fork
prong

first.

Bologna

First exposure to:

- Iceberg lettuce
- Potato chips
- White bread
- Mayonnaise

generated nausea like
bean curd soup, or,

1"-cubes of fried pork fat,
interspersed with 1mm.
lines of actual pink meat,
piled high on Moon Palace restaurant platters.

But, the round, rubbery bologna slices
my winking local butcher
gave me and Mei-Mei were
such treats. We'd

folded them into
pink, moist halfmoons—
nibbled their centers
with tiny un-
even teeth; looked at
each other through   peekaboo   keyholes;

winked at each other's giggling souls,
            wishing for piggyback rides into Candyland.

The Mouse

Squeal in the kitchenette
of Burgess Hall 4A

tiny furry thing
caught in the mousetrap;
my nine-year-old heart
skittered to a muffled stop

a tiny fistful of
grey cotton candy.

Grandmother's Kitchen

That dark unlit space,
a haven for my grandmother,
shuffling, groping
around for some odd,
forgotten thing—nothing
as handy, or American,
as Tupperware, nor
as concrete as that one
missing chopstick, but
necessary, nonetheless. Yet,

she'd managed
to pickle *oshinko* cucumbers
and eggplants, the *nuka-miso* stench
being her friend—to emerge from that dark,
unlikely space with a plate of ground beef omelet—
a miracle, considering her aversion to butter—
"*Bata-kusai,*" she'd mutter
about anything "Western" (I suppose my
white *gaijin* boyfriends reeked
of butter, too, like overfed geese). That

kitchen had been
her inviolate space that Banana
Yoshimoto would've praised to the white-
tiled skies (had it been visible)—*nuka-miso* reek
and incense fragrance intermingling in a pungent
vapory dance throughout that ramshackle two-
storied house in Suna-machi till my

mother modernized Grandmother's kitchen: she
flooded electric lights into it—plastered mildewed
     wood walls with pink rose vinyl wallpaper—crammed the latest
refrigerator model with
     meat and dairy products [blocks of *Yuki-Jirushi* butter] for me
and Mei-Mei, who'd
     grown into an American teenager in the porous City of Sand.

Since that kitchen makeover,
Grandmother would appear before us (while
we watched Madonna writhing
like a fallen snake goddess on MTV), kimono-less, muttering to herself,
her flattened-out, shriveled-up breasts exposed—
a grey specter we ignored. But, Mother
said *Obaa-chan* loved the new microwave
that steamed leftover rice to perfect white fluff.

Channel Surfers

Round and round the Japanese
TV frames flashed by—midsong
commercials—decapitated talking
heads—a whizzing jar of Shiseido
night cream in an amputated
hand—zap! long-haired screaming girl
running from a lumbering Texas chainsaw-
wielding…   zap! into psychedelic

Russian roulette repeat of commercial
chants; decapitated heads; amputated
hands—girl still screaming and
running—hair darkly plastered down
the skull of her head—abjected
spectacle fragments of ambivalent
voyeurism, for me and my kid sister
to resist, reject, regurgitate—compulsive
channel surfers, our screams over-
lapping with the girl's—wanting to
unplug, dump that TV into the murky
Sumida River oozing diarrheically—
beyond the bedroom terrace—after one
more round—just one more glimpse…
zap!

She Remains

Four days after *Hinamatsuri*, she became
that jeweled girl, five years before atomic bombs
shattered the oyster shell of her little
heart—and she grew
large breasts, and birthed two daughters,
(who replicated her without
the shell shock). She was

that child
cowering in the dark,
a spark, a tiny
nucleus of energy,
swollen
with tears,
postwar remnant
like the secret
gnawed potato
in scrawny
hands that would
nourish her into the solid,
buxom woman
she bloomed into, the PhD
being the consummation of all
that dark peeling away
from the kernel
of herself, leaving her

unscathed
and immaculate. She was
the pearl coalescing
in the grimacing oyster's mouth—
spitting her out—frothy iridescence,
rounded, and intact. Today,
I celebrate the woman
she is, as we spring forward into wilder bloom.
She remains

the photographer, (rather than the photograph);
the artist, (rather than the artifact);
at once, the signifier and the signified—
the wombed woman
suturing the wound within.

Mother's Garden

No secret garden, but
exhibited, instead, each
day on Facebook—different sprouts
and blooms each season:
cucumbers, snow peas, eggplants, zucchini, onions,
peaches, Cherokee purple and indigo rose tomatoes, bitter melon;

tulips, lilies, irises, lilac, pear tree blossom, crimson-
eyed rose of Sharon—precariously clambering trellis vines—potential
    harvest, unruined by chipmunks and invisible

insects speckling leaves,
wavering in sun and wind,
curling promises. Sunflowers

towered above me four summers ago,
in Mother's garden, their seedy, pockmarked faces nodding
golden approval. Each Mother's Day

memories (already captured) bloom along Facebook Timelines—
toward the heart's unravished harvest.

Umami

Essential component,
      a challenge to capture like slippery eel,
            yet to be broiled in soy sauce, sugar, and *mirin*
(think *unagi*). Umami,

the balance of all five flavors, countable on one hand:
sweet, salty, bitter, sour, spicy—
blending into one lovely flavor with the opening of buds—
the ripening of seasons—the precarious

balancing act—slippery
         acrobatics across the thick porous tongue.

Wei-Wei's Gift

Two birds and two roses emerged from
maroon paper after invisible scissors had snipped
away space—that intricate emergence;
framed medallion misnamed "paper

cut in China," as though paper-cut Chinese
fingers had bled a maroon trellis around
freeze-framed birds and roses—

an immaculate geometry.

Googling Monika

I never knew my German cousin
past the scrawny childhood
we both outgrew so rapidly—
nor her spectacled, gold-haired father,
photographed with her kimono-clad mother,
my Aunt Kuniko. Yet,

that intricate marital knot; that postwar
alliance between Axis powers
they'd beautifully embodied
promised to lift Aunt Kuniko from
dark cellars where potatoes were
stored, and secretly gnawed—
toward luminous, guttural realms,
where the obligatory *obi* would no longer cut
short her laughing breath. The fire and

ash of Auschwitz and Bergen-Belsen;
of Hiroshima and Nagasaki—are my cousin
Monika's twin legacies, folded into her
embroidered kimono sleeves, like over-
ripe persimmons. She

is the cousin who slipped through the cracks of
Grandmother's ramshackle Suna-machi house—
evaporating into rainbowed skies—now, intact,
and smiling on Google.

Additional Acknowledgments

The poems in *Epicanthus* affirm my Japanese American, and Taiwanese American, identity formation experiences that had yearned for articulation since my unforgettable encounter with Yuri Kochiyama in 1993, and since Marilyn Chin's inspirational IUWC poetry workshop in 2003. Thus, the process of writing these poems has enabled me to reclaim lost or complicated connections with family and East Asian cultures. In fact, when I look back at my forty discontinuous years of life in the United States of America, I imagine a palimpsest on which I glimpse fragments of my Japanese and Taiwanese girlhood selves behind opaque whitewash. And behind that tantalizing whitewash, I also discern the winking eye—one moment blue, then, brown—in either instance, the epicanthus being the divisive threshold that determines assimilation or exclusion in the USA. Resistance to civic exclusion is particularly urgent when Asian American voters require additional mobilization, even as anti-Asian racist acts fueled by the COVID-19 pandemic must be addressed. These are exceptional times that require the simultaneous erosion of divisive thresholds, and the reemergence of underrepresented experiences from behind the palimpsest whitewash of American life. Thus, these poems are readable as the products of such stringencies.

And so, for the possibility of these poems, I thank, once again, the organizers, instructors, and scholarship sponsors for the Indiana University Writers' Conference. My thanks extend to the Writers Guild at Bloomington for encouraging my work throughout these pandemic months. I gratefully acknowledge, in particular, the support of Tony Brewer, Dr. Joan Hawkins, Kyle Quass, Antonia Matthew, Eric Rensberger, and Nancy Chen Long. Special thanks to Patty Shin (*Gidra*), Traci Kato-Kiriyama (*Discover Nikkei*), and Stephanie Nguyen (Indiana University Bloomington) for enriching my writing experiences that are specifically Asian American.

My most precious thanks to my mother, Dr. Toyoko Yoshida, and to my sister, Tama Lang, to whom I have dedicated this book.

I thank all these wonderful individuals for standing with me at the epicanthic threshold, as we blink at the sun that did not mean to kill Icarus.

www.ingramcontent.com/pod-product-compliance
Lightning Source LLC
LaVergne TN
LVHW041553070426
835507LV00011B/1069